E-COMMERCE MASTERY: FROM ZERO TO SIX-FIGURE SALES IN JUST 6 MONTHS

A Step-by-Step Guide to Launching, Scaling, and Dominating Your Online Business

BY ALEX JORDAN

Copyright © ALEX JORDAN 2024.

All rights reserved. No part of this book may be reproduced, distributed, or transmitted in any form or by any means, including photocopying, recording, or other electronic or mechanical methods, without the prior written permission of the publisher, except in the case of brief quotations embodied in critical reviews and certain other noncommercial uses permitted by copyright law.

DEDICATION

To the dreamers and doers,

This book is dedicated to those who dare to envision a future beyond the conventional. To the entrepreneurs who relentlessly pursue their passions, and to the innovators who embrace change and challenge the status quo.

May your journey in the world of e-commerce be filled with growth, resilience, and endless possibilities. Your ambition and dedication inspire us all to reach for new heights.

With gratitude and admiration,

Alex Jordan

TABLE OF CONTENTS

1. Introduction

2. Getting Started

3. Setting Up Your Online Store

4. Product Sourcing and Inventory Management

5. Creating Compelling Product Listings

6. Building Your Brand

7. Driving Traffic to Your Store

8. Maximising Conversions

9. Leveraging Email Marketing

10. Utilising Content Marketing

11. Managing Customer Relationships

12. Analysing and Optimising Performance

13. Scaling Your Business

14. Legal and Financial Considerations

15. Case Studies and Success Stories

16. Conclusion

17. Resources and Further Reading

Bonus

Free Access to an E-Commerce Marketing Calendar Template

Thank You!

INTRODUCTION

Why E-Commerce?

In today's digital world, e-commerce has revolutionised the way we buy and sell goods and services all over the world. **But why choose e-commerce over traditional business methods?** The reasons are both compelling and numerous.

First and foremost, e-commerce offers unparalleled convenience. Consumers can shop from anywhere at any time, making it easier to fit shopping into their busy lives. This convenience extends to businesses as well, allowing entrepreneurs to reach a global audience without the limitations of a physical location.

Cost efficiency is another significant advantage. Starting an e-commerce business typically requires less capital compared to a brick-and-mortar store. There are no rental fees, and operational costs like utilities and staff can be minimised. Additionally, digital marketing often proves more affordable and effective than traditional advertising methods.

E-commerce also provides access to a vast amount of data and analytics. Business owners can track consumer behaviour, preferences, and purchasing patterns in real time. This data-driven approach allows for better decision-making, personalised marketing strategies, and improved customer experiences.

Moreover, e-commerce enables scalability. As your business grows, it's easier to expand your product range, enter new markets, and handle increased traffic without the significant overheads associated with physical expansion.

For essence, e-commerce is not just an alternative to traditional retail, it's a dynamic, flexible, and cost-effective way to build and grow a business in the modern world.

The Growth and Future of Online Business

The e-commerce industry has experienced exponential growth over the past decade, and its future looks even brighter. The rise of smartphones, improved internet connectivity, and advancements in technology has all contributed to this boom.

In the early days of the internet, e-commerce was primarily limited to large corporations with the resources to invest in online infrastructure. However, the development of user-friendly platforms like Shopify, WooCommerce, and Etsy has democratised e-commerce, allowing small businesses and individual entrepreneurs to set up shop online easily.

According to recent statistics, global e-commerce sales are expected to reach $6.38 trillion by 2024. This growth is driven by several factors, including the increasing popularity of mobile shopping, the expansion of the international markets, and the rise of social media as a powerful marketing tool.

The future of e-commerce will likely be shaped by innovations such as artificial intelligence (AI), augmented reality, and blockchain technology. AI can enhance customer service through chatbots and personalised recommendations. AR allows customers to virtually try products before purchasing, improving satisfaction and reducing returns. Blockchain can offer more secure and transparent transactions, boosting consumer trust.

Additionally, sustainable and ethical practices are becoming more important to consumers, and businesses that prioritise these values are likely to see increased loyalty and sales.

The growth and future of online business are marked by rapid advancements and expanding opportunities. E-commerce is set to continue its trajector, providing entrepreneurs with new ways to innovate, reach customers, and achieve success in the digital marketplaces.

GETTING STARTED

Identifying a Profitable Niche

One of the initial steps in building a successful e-commerce business is identifying a profitable niche. A niche is a specialised segment of the market that caters to a specific audience with distinct needs or preferences. Finding the right niche is crucial because it helps you stand out in a crowded market and attract a loyal customer base.

1. Assess Your Interests and Expertise: Start by making a list of topics or industries you are passionate about or have knowledge in. Running a business around something you love or understand well will keep you motivated and give you an edge over competitors who might not have the same level of passion or expertise like you.

2. Analyse Market Demand: Use tools like Google Trends, Amazon Best Sellers, and keyword research tools to gauge the demand for your potential niches.

Look for niches with steady or growing interest over time. High demand indicates a larger audience and more potential for sales.

3. Evaluate Competition: While competition can indicate a healthy market, too much of it might make it difficult for you to break through. Look for niches that are not overly saturated. Tools like SEMrush and Ahrefs can help you analyse the competitive landscape by showing how many businesses are already targeting your chosen niche.

4. Identify Pain Points and Gaps: Search online forums, social media groups, and customer reviews to identify common pain points or gaps in the market. Look for problems that are not being adequately addressed by existing businesses. This can help you position your product or service as a unique solution.

5. Consider Profit Margins: Calculate the potential profit margins for products in your chosen niche. Consider factors like production costs, shipping fees, and pricing strategies. Higher profit margins can give you more flexibility in your marketing and business operations.

By carefully evaluating these factors, you can identify a niche that is not only profitable but also aligned with your interests and expertise, setting a strong foundation for your e-commerce business.

Conducting Market Research

Once you have identified a potential niche, the next step is to conduct thorough market research. This involves gathering information about your target audience, competitors, and overall market trends to make informed decisions.

1. Define Your Target Audience: Create detailed buyer personas that represent your ideal customers. Consider factors like age, gender, location, income level, interests, and shopping behaviour. Understanding your target audience will help you tailor your marketing messages and product offerings to meet their needs.

2. Analyse Competitors: Identify your main competitors and analyse their strengths and weaknesses. Look at their product offerings, pricing strategies, marketing tactics, and customer reviews. Tools like SimilarWeb and SpyFu can provide insights into your competitors' online presence and performance.

3. Survey Potential Customers: Use surveys and questionnaires to gather direct feedback from potential customers. Ask about their preferences, pain points, and purchasing habits. This can provide valuable insights into what they are looking for and how you can meet their needs better than your competitors.

SETTING UP YOUR ONLINE STORE

Choosing the Right E-Commerce Platform

Selecting the right e-commerce platform is important for the success of your online store. The platform you choose will serve as the foundation for your business, so it's important to pick one that aligns with your needs and goals.

1. Assess Your Business Needs: Start by listing your business requirements. Consider factors like the size of your inventory, the complexity of your product offerings, your budget, and your technical expertise. Some platforms are better suited for small businesses with a limited product range, while others can handle large, complex inventories.

2. Popular E-Commerce Platforms:
- **Shopify:** Known for its user-friendliness and robust features, Shopify is a great choice for beginners and

small to medium-sized businesses. It offers a wide range of themes, apps, and integrations, making it easy to customise your store.

- **WooCommerce:** This is a WordPress plugin that allows you to turn your WordPress site into an e-commerce store. It's highly customizable and ideal for those who are familiar with WordPress.
- **BigCommerce** is known for its scalability and powerful built-in features. It's suitable for businesses of all sizes, especially those planning to grow quickly.
- **Magento:** A more advanced platform, Magento offers extensive customization options and is suitable for larger businesses with complex needs. It requires technical knowledge to set up and maintain.
- **Wix eCommerce:** Ideal for small businesses and entrepreneurs who need a simple and intuitive platform. Wix offers a drag-and-drop interface and various templates to get you started quickly.

3. Ease of Use: Ensure the platform you choose is easy to use and manage. Look for platforms that offer intuitive interfaces, drag-and-drop builders, and comprehensive customer support. The easier the platform to use, the more time you can spend focusing on growing your business.

4. Cost: Evaluate the pricing plans of different platforms. Some may have a low monthly fee but charge additional transaction fees, while others might offer all-inclusive plans. Choose a platform that fits within your budget and provides good value for money.

5. Scalability: Consider your future growth. Choose a platform that can scale with your business, offering advanced features and higher performance as your store grows.

6. Integrations and Plugins: Check if the platform supports integrations with other tools and services you might need, such as payment gateways, email marketing tools, and analytics software. The more integrations available, the easier it will be to manage your business.

Designing Your Store for Success

The design of your online store plays a crucial role in attracting and retaining customers. A well-designed store not only looks professional but also provides a seamless shopping experience.

1. Choose a Professional Theme: Most e-commerce platforms offer a variety of themes and templates to choose from. Select a theme that aligns with your brand's aesthetic and provides a good user experience. Ensure it is mobile-friendly, as a significant portion of online shopping is done on mobile devices.

2. User-Friendly Navigation: Makes it easy for customers to find what they're looking for. Organize your products into clear categories, use straightforward menu structures, and include a search bar. The easier it is to navigate your store, the more likely customers are to make a purchase.

3. High-Quality Images: Use high-quality images for your products. Clear, detailed photos help customers see exactly what they're buying, which can reduce returns and increase customer satisfaction. Consider using multiple images from different angles and including zoom functionality.

4. Compelling Product Descriptions: Write detailed and persuasive product descriptions. Highlight the features and benefits of each product, and include any relevant specifications. Use bullet points to make the information easy to scan.

5. Trust Signals: Build trust with your customers by including trust signals on your site. This can include customer reviews, testimonials, security badges, and clear return policies. Trust signals reassure customers that your site is safe and reliable.

6. Clear Call-to-Actions : Use clear and compelling CTAs to guide customers through the buying process. Buttons like "Add to Cart," "Buy Now," and "Checkout" should stand out and be easy to find.

7. Fast Loading Times: Ensure your site loads quickly. Slow loading times can frustrate customers and lead to higher bounce rates. Optimise your images and use a reliable hosting service to keep your site running smoothly.

8. Checkout Process: Simplify the checkout process to reduce cart abandonment. Use as few steps as possible, offer multiple payment options, and allow guest checkout. Make sure the process is secure and straightforward.

Essential Tools and Plugins

To run a successful e-commerce store, you'll need various tools and plugins to enhance functionality and streamline operations.

1. Payment Gateways: Integrate reliable payment gateways to accept payments securely. Popular options include PayPal, Stripe, Square, and Authorize.Net. Offering multiple payment options can increase conversion rates by accommodating customer preferences.

2. SEO Tools: Use SEO tools to optimise your store for search engines. Plugins like Yoast SEO (for WordPress) or built-in SEO features in Shopify and BigCommerce can help you improve your search engine rankings, driving more organic traffic to your site.

3. Email Marketing: Integrate email marketing tools like Mailchimp, Klaviyo, or Constant Contact to stay in touch with your customers. Use these tools to send newsletters, promotional offers, and abandoned cart reminders.

4. Analytics: Use analytics tools to track your store's performance. Google Analytics is a must-have for understanding your traffic sources, customer behaviour, and sales data. Many e-commerce platforms also offer built-in analytics dashboards.

5. Inventory Management: Manage your stock levels efficiently with inventory management tools. Apps like TradeGecko, Zoho Inventory, or built-in features in platforms like Shopify can help you keep track of your inventory and avoid stockouts or overstocking.

6. Customer Support: Offer excellent customer support with tools like Zendesk, LiveChat, or Help Scout. Providing timely and helpful support can improve customer satisfaction and loyalty.

7. Social Media Integration: Integrate your store with social media platforms to drive traffic and sales. Tools like Buffer or Hootsuite can help you manage your social media presence and schedule posts.

8. Reviews and Ratings: Encourage customers to leave reviews and ratings with tools like Yotpo or

Trustpilot. Positive reviews build trust and can significantly influence potential customers' purchasing decisions.

Setting up your online store involves a careful planning and execution. By choosing the right e-commerce platform, designing a user friendly and attractive store, and utilising essential tools and plugins, you can create a strong foundation for your e-commerce business. This will help you attract customers, drive sales, and grow your business in the competitive online marketplace.

4. Examine Industry Trends: Stay updated on the latest trends and developments in your industry. Follow industry blogs, attend webinars, and participate in online communities to gain insights into emerging trends and technologies. This can help you stay ahead of the curve and adapt to your business strategy accordingly.

5. Test Your Ideas: Before fully committing to a niche, consider running small-scale tests to validate your ideas. This could involve setting up a simple landing page, running a limited ads campaign, or launching a pilot product. Monitor the results and gather feedback to refine your approach.

Conducting thorough market research will help you make informed decisions, minimise risks, and increase your chances of success in the e-commerce space.

Crafting Your Unique Value Proposition

Your unique value proposition (UVP) is a clear statement that explains how your product or service solves your customers' problems or improves their situation, delivers specific benefits, and tells the customer why they should buy from you instead of your competitors. A strong UVP is essential for differentiating your business and attracting your target audience.

1. Identify Your Key Benefits: Start by listing the main benefits your product or service offers. These should be benefits that are important to your target audience and address their specific needs or pain points. Focus on what makes your offering unique and valuable.

2. Highlight Your Differentiators: Determine what sets your business apart from the competition. This could be anything from superior quality, innovative features, exceptional customer service, or a unique brand story. Highlighting these differentiators will help you stand out in a crowded market.

3. Craft a Clear and Compelling Message: Your UVP should be concise, clear, and compelling. Avoid jargon and focus on delivering a straightforward message that resonates with your audience. Use simple language that clearly communicates the value you offer.

4. Incorporate Your UVP into Your Branding: Ensure that your UVP is reflected in all aspects of your branding, from your website and marketing materials to your product packaging and customer interactions. Consistency in messaging will help reinforce your value proposition and build trust with your audience.

5. Test and Refine Your UVP: Once you have crafted your UVP, test it with your target audience. Gather feedback to see if it resonates and makes sense to them. Use this feedback to refine and improve your UVP over time.

An effective UVP will not only attract potential customers but also help you build a loyal customer base by clearly communicating the unique value you offer.

Getting started with your e-commerce business involves identifying a profitable niche, conducting thorough market research, and crafting a compelling unique value proposition. By following these steps, you can set a strong foundation for your business, differentiate yourself from the competition, and position yourself for long-term success in the dynamic world of e-commerce.

PRODUCT SOURCING AND INVENTORY MANAGEMENT

Finding Reliable Suppliers

The success of your e-commerce business greatly depends on finding reliable suppliers who can provide quality products at competitive prices. Here's how you can find and choose the best suppliers for your business.

1. Research and Identify Potential Suppliers: Start by conducting thorough research to identify potential suppliers. You can use online directories like Alibaba, Global Sources, and ThomasNet, which list thousands of manufacturers and wholesalers. Attending trade shows and industry events can also help you meet suppliers in person and build relationships.

2. Evaluate Supplier Reliability: Once you have a list of potential suppliers, evaluate their reliability. Check their reputation by looking at customer reviews, ratings, and feedback. A reliable supplier will have positive reviews and a good track record of delivering quality products on time.

3. Request Samples: Before committing to a supplier, request product samples. This allows you to assess the quality of their products firsthand. It's important to test multiple samples to ensure consistency in quality.

4. Negotiate Terms and Prices: After you're satisfied with the product quality, negotiate terms and prices with the supplier. Discuss payment terms, minimum order quantities, lead times, and shipping options. Building a good relationship with your supplier can help you negotiate better terms.

5. Check for Certifications and Compliance: Ensure that the supplier complies with industry standards and regulations. Ask for certifications or proof of compliance, especially if you're sourcing products that need to meet specific safety or quality standards.

6. Start with a Small Order: When working with a new supplier, start with a small order to minimise risk. This allows you to test their reliability and the quality of their products without making a significant investment.

Managing Inventory Efficiently

Efficient inventory management is crucial for maintaining a healthy cash flow, minimising storage costs, and ensuring you can meet customer demand. Here are some tips for effective inventory management.

1. Use Inventory Management Software: Invest in reliable inventory management software like TradeGecko, Zoho Inventory, or the built-in tools provided by your e-commerce platform. These tools help you track stock levels, manage orders, and forecast demand.

2. Set Reorder Points: Determine the minimum stock level for each product, known as the reorder point. When inventory falls below this level, it's time to reorder. This helps prevent stockouts and ensures you always have enough inventory to meet customer demand.

3. Regularly Review Inventory Levels: Conduct regular inventory audits to ensure the accuracy of your stock levels. This can be done through physical counts or using automated systems. Regular reviews help identify discrepancies and prevent overstocking or stockouts.

4. Implement Just-In-Time (JIT) Inventory: JIT inventory management involves ordering products only when they are needed for sale. This reduces the amount of inventory you need to store and minimises storage costs. However, it requires reliable suppliers and efficient logistics to avoid delays.

5. Use ABC Analysis: ABC analysis helps prioritise inventory management efforts by categorising products based on their importance. 'A' items are high-value products with low sales frequency, 'B' items are moderate value with moderate sales frequency, and 'C' items are low-value with high sales frequency. Focus more on managing 'A' items as they have the most significant impact on your business.

6. Forecast Demand: Use historical sales data and market trends to forecast future demand. Accurate demand forecasting helps you maintain optimal inventory levels, reduce excess stock, and prevent stockouts.

Dropshipping vs. Holding Inventory

Choosing between dropshipping and holding inventory depends on your business model, budget, and goals. Here's a comparison of both methods to help you decide on which is best for you:

1. **Dropshipping:**
   - **Advantages:**
     - Lower Startup Costs: Dropshipping eliminates the need for purchasing and storing inventory upfront, reducing initial costs.
     - Reduced Risk: Since you only purchase products after a customer places an order, there's less financial risk associated with unsold inventory.

- Easy to Scale: Dropshipping allows you to scale your business quickly as you don't have to worry about managing large inventories or logistics.

• Disadvantages:
- Lower Profit Margins: Since you're buying products individually from suppliers, the cost per unit is higher, resulting in lower profit margins.
- Less Control Over Quality and Shipping: Relying on suppliers for order fulfilment means you have less control over product quality and shipping times, which can affect customer satisfaction.
- Competition: Dropshipping is a popular business model, leading to high competition and price wars.

2. **Holding Inventory:**

• Advantages:
- Higher Profit Margins: Buying products in bulk allows you to negotiate better prices, resulting in higher profit margins.
- Better Control Over Quality and Shipping: Managing your inventory gives you complete control over product quality and shipping times, enhancing customer satisfaction.
- Branding Opportunities: Holding inventory allows you to customise packaging and include branded materials, improving your brand's image and customer experience.

• Disadvantages:
- Higher Startup Costs: Purchasing inventory upfront and storing it requires a significant initial investment.

- Storage and Handling Costs: Managing inventory involves costs for storage, handling, and potential losses due to damage or obsolescence.
- Risk of Unsold Inventory: There's a financial risk associated with unsold inventory, especially if market demand changes or products become obsolete.

Effective product sourcing and inventory management are critical components of a successful e-commerce business. By finding reliable suppliers, managing your inventory efficiently, and choosing the right fulfilment method, you can ensure smooth operations, satisfy customer demand, and maximise profitability. Whether you opt for dropshipping or holding inventory, understanding the advantages and disadvantages of each approach will help you make informed decisions that align with your business goals.

CREATING COMPELLING PRODUCT LISTINGS

Writing Persuasive Product Descriptions

A compelling product description is crucial for converting visitors into buyers. It should provide essential information, highlight key benefits, and persuade customers to make a purchase. Here are some tips for writing persuasive product descriptions:

1. Know Your Audience: Understand who your target customers are and what they value. Tailor your language and tone to resonate with them. For example, a technical savvy audience might appreciate detailed specifications, while a fashion-focused audience might be more interested in style and appearance.

2. Focus on Benefits, Not Just Features: While it's important to list the features of your product, emphasise how those features benefit the customer. For example, instead of saying "This blender has a 500-watt motor," say "Blend smoothies quickly and effortlessly with the powerful 500-watt motor."

3. Use Engaging Language: Use descriptive and engaging language to make your product come alive. Words like "luxurious," "sleek," "innovative," and "durable" can create a vivid picture in the customer's mind.

4. Keep It Clear and Concise: While being descriptive, avoid lengthy paragraphs. Use bullet points to highlight key features and benefits. This makes the description easier to scan and understand quickly.

5. Incorporate Keywords for SEO: Use relevant keywords naturally within your product description to improve your search engine rankings. This helps potential customers find your products more easily.

6. Tell a Story: Where appropriate, tell a story about your product. Explain how it was developed, its inspiration, or how it can fit into the customer's life. Stories can create an emotional connection with your audience.

7. Include a Call to Action (CTA): Encourage customers to take the next step with a clear and compelling CTA. Phrases like "Buy Now," "Add to Cart," or "Get Yours Today" can prompt immediate action.

High-Quality Product Photography

High-quality images are essential for showcasing your products and convincing customers to buy. Here are some tips for creating effective product photography:

1. Use Good Lighting: Natural light is often the best for product photography. Shoot near a window or use softbox lighting to eliminate harsh shadows and highlight your product's features.

2. Choose the Right Background: A clean, simple background ensures that the focus remains on your product. White or neutral backgrounds are common, but you can use coloured or textured backgrounds if they complement your product and brand.

3. Show Multiple Angles: Provide images from various angles to give customers a comprehensive view of the product. Include close-ups of important details and features.

4. Show the Product in Use: Lifestyle photos showing the product in use can help customers visualise how it fits into their lives. For example, show a model wearing the clothing or a person using the kitchen gadget.

5. Maintain Consistency: Ensure consistency in your photography style across all products. This includes lighting, background, and image size. Consistency helps create a professional and cohesive look for your store.

6. Use High Resolution: High-resolution images look more professional and allow customers to zoom in to see details. Ensure your images are clear and sharp.

7. Edit Your Photos: Use photo editing software to enhance your images. Adjust brightness, contrast, and colour balance to make your product look its best. However, avoid over-editing, which can mislead customers about the product's true appearance.

8. Include Size and Scale: Show the scale of your product by including an object for reference or by using a model. This helps customers understand the actual size and reduces the risk of returns due to size misinterpretations.

Pricing Strategies

Pricing your products correctly is essential for attracting customers and maintaining profitability. Here are some pricing strategies to consider:

1. Cost-Plus Pricing: Calculate the cost of producing your product and add a markup to ensure a profit. This straightforward approach ensures you cover your costs and achieve your desired profit margin.

2. Competitive Pricing: Research your competitors' prices and set your prices accordingly. You can choose to match, undercut, or slightly exceed their prices depending on your positioning and value proposition.

3. **Value-Based Pricing:** Price your products based on the perceived value to the customer rather than the cost. If your product offers unique features or benefits that set it apart, customers may be willing to pay more.

4. **Psychological Pricing:** Use pricing techniques that appeal to customers' psychology. Common methods include pricing items just below a round number (e.g., $9.99 instead of $10.00) and offering tiered pricing (example, basic, standard, and premium options).

5. **Discounts and Promotions:** Offer discounts, sales, or promotional pricing to attract customers and boost sales. Limited-time offers can create a sense of urgency, encouraging customers to buy now.

6. **Bundling:** Combine several products and sell them at a reduced price compared to buying each item individually. Bundling can increase the perceived value and encourage customers to spend more.

7. **Freemium Model:** Offer a basic version of your product for free and charge for premium features. This model is common in digital products and services, allowing customers to try before they buy.

8. **Dynamic Pricing:** Adjust your prices based on demand, competition, and other factors. This approach

is common in industries like travel and event ticketing but can be applied to e-commerce with the right tools.

Creating compelling product listings involves writing persuasive product descriptions, using high-quality product photography, and employing effective pricing strategies. By focusing on these key elements, you can attract more customers, increase sales, and build a successful e-commerce business. Understanding your audience, presenting your products in the best light, and setting competitive yet profitable prices will help you stand out in the crowded online marketplace.

BUILDING YOUR BRAND

Developing a Strong Brand Identity

Creating a strong brand identity is the foundation of a successful business. Your brand identity defines who you are, what you stand for, and how you want to be perceived by your customers. Here are the key steps to developing a robust brand identity:

1. Define Your Brand's Purpose and Values: Start by clearly defining the purpose of your brand. Ask yourself why your brand exists, what problems it solves, and what values it upholds. Your brand's purpose and values should resonate with your target audience and differentiate you from competitors.

2. Understand Your Target Audience: Know who your customers are, their needs, preferences, and pain points. Create detailed buyer personas that represent your ideal customers. Understanding your audience helps tailor your brand identity to meet their expectations and build stronger connections.

3. Analyse Your Competitors: Conduct a thorough analysis of your competitors to identify their strengths, weaknesses, and branding strategies. This will help you find gaps in the market and opportunities to position your brand uniquely.

4. Develop Your Brand's Personality: Your brand's personality should reflect the characteristics and qualities you want to be associated with your brand. Decide on a tone of voice and communication style that aligns with your brand's values and resonates with your audience. Is your brand friendly and approachable, professional and authoritative, or innovative and edgy?

5. Create a Unique Selling Proposition (USP): Your USP is what sets you apart from the competition. It's the unique benefit or value that your brand offers. Ensure that your USP is clear, compelling, and easily communicated to your customers.

Creating a Memorable Logo and Brand Story

A memorable logo and a compelling brand story are essential components of your brand identity. They help create a visual and emotional connection with your audience.

1. Designing Your Logo:

Simplicity: A simple logo is easily recognizable and memorable. Avoid complex designs that can confuse or overwhelm your audience.

Relevance: Your logo should reflect your brand's values, industry, and personality. Use symbols, colours, and fonts that align with your brand identity.

Versatility: Ensure your logo looks good in different sizes and formats, from business cards to billboards. It should also work in both colour and black-and-white versions.

Timelessness: Aim for a logo design that can stand the test of time. Avoid trends that might become outdated quickly.

Feedback and Refinement: Get feedback from your target audience and refine your logo based on their input. This ensures your logo resonates with the people who matter most.

2. Crafting Your Brand Story:

Origin: Share the story of how and why your brand was founded. Highlight the challenges, motivations, and inspirations behind its creation.

Mission and Vision: Clearly state your brand's mission (what you aim to achieve) and vision (the future you envision). This helps customers understand your long-term goals and aspirations.

Core Values: Outline the core values that guide your brand's actions and decisions. These values should be reflected in everything you do and communicate.

Customer Impact: Highlight how your brand makes a positive impact on your customers' lives. Use real stories and testimonials to illustrate this impact.

Emotional Connection: Create an emotional connection by sharing relatable and humanising aspects of your brand story. Emotions drive customer loyalty and advocacy.

Consistent Brand Messaging

Consistency in brand messaging is crucial for building trust and recognition. It ensures that your brand communicates the same message across all touchpoints and interactions.

1. Develop a Brand Messaging Framework: Create a comprehensive brand messaging framework that includes your brand's mission, vision, values, and key messages. This framework should serve as a guide for all your communications.

2. Define Your Brand Voice and Tone:

- **Voice:** Your brand voice is the consistent personality and style of communication. It should be aligned with your brand's identity and resonate with your audience.
- **Tone:** Your tone can vary depending on the context and medium. For example, your tone might be more formal in a press release but friendly and conversational on social media. Ensure the tone always aligns with your brand voice.

3. Maintain Visual Consistency: Consistent visual elements, such as colours, fonts, and imagery, reinforce your brand identity. Use a brand style guide to ensure all visual materials are cohesive and aligned with your brand's aesthetics.

4. Use Consistent Messaging Across Channels: Whether it's your website, social media, emails, or advertisements, ensure that your brand messaging is consistent across all channels. This helps build a unified and recognizable brand image.

5. Train Your Team: Educate your team about your brand identity and messaging framework. Ensure everyone understands and adheres to the brand guidelines. Consistency from all team members strengthens the overall brand.

6. Monitor and Adjust: Regularly monitor your brand messaging and gather feedback from your audience. Adjust your messaging as needed to stay relevant and resonant with your target customers.

Building a strong brand involves developing a clear and compelling brand identity, creating a memorable logo and brand story, to ensure consistent brand messaging. By defining your brand's purpose, understanding your audience, and differentiating yourself from competitors, you can create a brand that resonates with customers and stands out in the market. Consistency in your visual and verbal communication further strengthens your brand, fostering trust and loyalty among your audience. These efforts combined will help you build a powerful and lasting brand that drives your business's success.

DRIVING TRAFFIC TO YOUR STORE

Search Engine Optimization (SEO) for E-Commerce

SEO is a critical component of driving organic traffic to your e-commerce store. By optimising your website for search engines, you can improve your visibility and attract potential customers who are searching for products you offer. Here's how to effectively implement SEO for your e-commerce store:

1. Keyword Research: Identify relevant keywords that potential customers use to search for products. Use tools like Google Keyword Planner, Ahrefs, or SEMrush to find high-volume, low-competition keywords. Focus on long-tail keywords that are more specific and have a higher intent to purchase.

2. On-Page SEO:
   •**Title Tags and Meta Descriptions:** Craft compelling title tags and meta descriptions that include your target keywords. These elements appear in search engine results and can influence click-through rates.

- **Product Descriptions:** Write unique, detailed, and keyword-rich product descriptions. Avoid duplicate content, as it can harm your search rankings. Include key features, benefits, and use cases of your products.
- **URL Structure:** Use clean, descriptive URLs that include relevant keywords. Avoid using long strings of numbers or irrelevant characters.
- **Header Tags:** Use header tags (H1, H2, H3) to structure your content. Incorporate your target keywords naturally into these headings to improve readability and SEO.

3. Technical SEO:

- **Site Speed:** Ensure your website loads quickly. Use tools like Google PageSpeed Insights to identify and fix performance issues.
- **Mobile-Friendliness:** Optimise your site for mobile devices. Google prioritises mobile-friendly websites in its search rankings.
- **SSL Certificate:** Secure your site with an SSL certificate (HTTPS). This not only protects user data but also boosts your search rankings.
- **XML Sitemap:** Create and submit an XML sitemap to search engines. This helps them index your pages more effectively.

4. Content Marketing:

Create valuable, informative, and engaging content that attracts your target audience. Blog posts, how-to guides, and product reviews can drive organic traffic and establish your authority in your niche. Incorporate keywords naturally into your content and promote it through social media and email marketing.

5. Backlinks: Earn high-quality backlinks from reputable websites in your industry. Backlinks are a strong ranking factor for search engines. Reach out to bloggers, influencers, and industry publications for guest posting opportunities or product reviews.

Pay-Per-Click Advertising (PPC)

PPC advertising allows you to drive targeted traffic to your e-commerce store quickly. With PPC, you pay only when someone clicks on your ad. Here's how to effectively use PPC advertising:

1. Choose the Right Platforms: Google Ads and Bing Ads are popular search engine advertising platforms. For social media PPC, consider Facebook Ads, Instagram Ads, and Pinterest Ads, depending on where your target audience spends their time.

2. Keyword Targeting: Conduct thorough keyword research to identify the best keywords for your PPC campaigns. Use tools like Google Ads Keyword Planner to find high-converting keywords. Focus on both broad and long-tail keywords to capture a wider audience.

3. Ad Copy: Write a compelling ads copy that grabs attention and encourages clicks. Highlight unique selling points, promotions, and benefits. Use strong calls to action like "Shop Now," "Buy Today," or "Get Yours Now."

4. Landing Pages: Ensure your landing pages are optimised for conversions. The landing page should match the ad's message and offer. Include clear headlines, engaging visuals, product details, and a prominent CTA. A/B test different landing page elements to improve performance.

5. Bid Management: Set your bid strategy based on your campaign goals. Manual CPC bidding allows you to control your bids for specific keywords, while automated bidding strategies like target CPA (Cost Per Acquisition) can help maximise conversions within your budget.

6. Ads Extensions: Use ad extensions to provide additional information and improve ad visibility. Extensions like site link, callout, and structured snippet extensions can enhance your ads and increase click-through rates.

7. Monitor and Optimise: Regularly monitor your PPC campaigns to track performance. Use metrics like click-through rate (CTR), conversion rate, and return on ad spend (ROAS) to evaluate effectiveness. Optimise your campaigns by adjusting bids, refining keywords, and improving ad copy and landing pages.

Social Media Marketing

Social media marketing is a powerful way to drive traffic to your e-ecommerce store, engage with your audience, and build brand loyalty. Here's how to leverage social media for your business:

1. Choose the Right Platforms: Focus on the social media platforms where your target audience is most active. Facebook, Instagram, Twitter, Pinterest, and LinkedIn are popular options for e-commerce businesses.

2. Create Engaging Content:
   •**Visual Content:** Use high-quality images, videos, and graphics to showcase your products. Visual content is more engaging and shareable than text-only posts.
   •**User-Generated Content:** Encourage customers to share photos and reviews of your products. Feature user-generated content on your social media channels to build trust and authenticity.
   •**Storytelling:** Share behind-the-scenes stories, brand history, and customer success stories. Storytelling helps create an emotional connection with your audience.

3. Consistent Posting Schedule: Maintain a consistent posting schedule to keep your audience engaged. Use social media management tools like Buffer, Hootsuite, or Sprout Social to plan and schedule your posts.

4. Influencer Marketing: Collaborate with influencers in your niche to reach a larger audience. Influencers can create authentic content that promotes your products and drives traffic to your store. Choose influencers whose followers match your target audience.

5. Social Media Advertising: Use paid social media ads to boost your reach and drive targeted traffic. Platforms like Facebook and Instagram offer advanced targeting options based on demographics, interests, and behaviors. Create eye-catching ads with compelling CTAs to encourage clicks and conversions.

6. Engage with Your Audience: Respond to comments, messages, and mentions promptly. Engaging with your audience builds trust and encourages them to interact with your brand. Host Q&A sessions, live videos, and contests to foster engagement.

7. Analyse and Optimize: Track your social media performance using analytics tools provided by each platform. Monitor metrics like engagement rate, reach, and website traffic. Use these insights to refine your social media strategy and improve results.

Driving traffic to your e-commerce store requires a multifaceted approach that includes SEO, PPC advertising, and social media marketing. By optimising your website for search engines, you can attract organic traffic from users searching for products you offer. PPC advertising provides a quick and effective way to drive targeted traffic, while social media marketing helps you engage with your audience and build brand loyalty. By implementing these strategies, you can increase your store's visibility, attract more customers, and ultimately boost your sales.

MAXIMISING CONVERSIONS

Optimising the Customer Journey

Optimising the customer journey involves creating a seamless and enjoyable experience from the moment a potential customer discovers your store to the point of purchase. Here are key strategies to optimise the customer journey effectively:

1. User Friendly Website Design: Ensure your website is easy to navigate. Use a clean, intuitive layout with clear categories and search functionality. Make it easy for visitors to find products, access their shopping cart, and complete purchases. A well-designed website enhances user experience and reduces bounce rates.

2. Mobile Optimisation: With the increasing use of mobile devices for online shopping, it's crucial to have a mobile-friendly website. Ensure your site is responsive, meaning it adapts to different screen sizes and provides a smooth browsing experience on smartphones and tablets.

3. Fast Loading Times: Slow loading times can frustrate users and lead to high bounce rates. Optimise your site's performance by compressing images, using efficient coding practices, and leveraging content delivery networks (CDNs). Aim for a load time of under three seconds.

4. Clear Product Pages: Design product pages with clear and detailed information. Include high-quality images, comprehensive descriptions, customer reviews, and pricing details. The more information customers have, the more confident they feel about their purchase.

5. Simplified Checkout Process: Reduce cart abandonment by streamlining the checkout process. Minimise the number of steps required to complete a purchase, offer guest checkout options, and provide multiple payment methods. Display trust signals, such as secure payment icons, to reassure customers.

6. Personalisation: Use data to personalise the shopping experience. Recommend products based on browsing history, previous purchases, or customer preferences. Personalisation can increase engagement and encourage repeat purchases.

7. Customer Support: Provide accessible customer support options, such as live chat, email, and phone support. Addressing customer queries and concerns promptly can improve satisfaction and increase conversions.

8. Retargeting: Implement retargeting strategies to re-engage visitors who left your site without making a purchase. Use personalised ads and email campaigns to remind them of products they viewed and encourage them to return and complete their purchase.

Effective Call-to-Actions (CTAs)

CTAs are essential for guiding customers towards desired actions, such as adding items to their cart, signing up for newsletters, or completing a purchase. Here's how to create effective CTAs:

1. Be Clear and Direct: Your CTA should clearly state what action you want the customer to take. Use concise, action-oriented language. Phrases like "Buy Now," "Add to Cart," "Subscribe," or "Get Started" leave no room for confusion.

2. Create a Sense of Urgency: Encourage immediate action by incorporating urgency into your CTAs. Phrases like "Limited Time Offer," "Shop Now While Supplies Last," or "Order Today for Free Shipping" can prompt customers to act quickly.

3. Use Contrasting Colours: Make your CTAs stand out by using colours that contrast with the rest of the page. This draws attention to the CTA button and makes it more likely that users will click on it.

4. Position Strategically: Place CTAs in prominent positions where they are easily noticed. Common placements include above the fold on product pages, at the end of blog posts, and in the header or footer of your site.

5. Test Different Variations: Experiment with different CTA texts, colours, sizes, and placements to see what works best. A/B testing can help you determine which variations yield the highest conversion rates.

6. Use First-Person Language: Personalising CTAs with first-person language can make them more compelling. For example, "Start My Free Trial" instead of "Start Your Free Trial" can create a stronger connection with the customer.

7. Highlight Benefits: Emphasise the benefits of taking action. Instead of just "Sign Up," try "Sign Up for Exclusive Discounts" or "Get Instant Access to Our Best Deals." Highlighting the value proposition can make the CTA more attractive.

A/B Testing for Better Results

A/B testing, or split testing, is a method of comparing two versions of a webpage or element to determine which one performs better. Here's how to use A/B testing to maximise conversions:

1. Identify Testing Elements: Choose the elements you want to test. These could include headlines, CTA buttons, product images, page layouts, or pricing displays. Focus on one element at a time to get clear results.

2. Create Variations: Develop two versions of the element you're testing the original (control) and a modified version (variation). Ensure the changes are significant enough to potentially impact user behaviour.

3. Set Clear Goals: Define what you want to achieve with the A/B test. Common goals include increasing click-through rates, reducing bounce rates, or boosting conversion rates. Clear goals help you measure the success of the test accurately.

4. Split Your Audience: Divide your audience randomly into two groups. One group sees the control version, while the other sees the variation. This random distribution helps ensure that the results are not biassed.

5. Run the Test for a Sufficient Period: Allow the test to run long enough to gather meaningful data. Running the test for at least a week can account for variations in user behaviour across different days and times.

6. Analyse the Results: Use statistical analysis to determine which version performed better. Look at metrics like conversion rate, click-through rate, and engagement time. Tools like Google Optimise, Optimizely, and VWO can help with analysis.

7. Implement the Winning Variation: If the variation outperforms the control, implement the changes permanently. If the control performs better, consider testing a different variation or element.

8. Continuous Testing: A/B testing is an ongoing process. Continuously test different elements of your site to keep improving user experience and conversions. Regular testing helps you stay adaptable to changing customer preferences and market trends.

Maximising conversions requires a strategic approach to optimising the customer journey, crafting effective CTAs, and employing A/B testing. By focusing on user-friendly design, mobile optimisation, fast loading times, clear product pages, simplified checkout, personalisation, customer support, and retargeting, you can create a seamless and engaging customer experience. Effective CTAs guide users toward desired actions with clarity, urgency, contrasting colors, strategic placement, first-person language, and benefit highlighting. A/B testing allows you to make data-driven decisions to continually enhance your site's performance. Together, these strategies can significantly boost your conversion rates and drive the success of your e-commerce business.

LEVERAGING EMAIL MARKETING

Email marketing is a powerful tool for engaging with your audience, nurturing leads, and driving sales. Here's how to effectively leverage email marketing for your e-commerce business:

Building an Email List

1. Offer Valuable Incentives: To encourage visitors to subscribe to your email list, offer something of value in return. This could be a discount on their first purchase, a free ebook, access to exclusive content, or entry into a giveaway. The incentive should be compelling enough to motivate users to provide their email addresses.

2. Create Opt-In Forms: Place opt-in forms strategically throughout your website. Common locations include the homepage, blog posts, pop-ups, and the checkout page. Keep the forms simple and only ask for essential information (e.g., name and email address) to reduce friction.

3. Leverage Social Media: Promote your email newsletter on your social media platforms. Use posts and ads to highlight the benefits of subscribing.

Consider running social media contests where users must subscribe to your email list to participate.

4. Use Exit-Intent Pop-Ups: Exit-intent pop-ups appear when a user is about to leave your website. These pop-ups can offer a last-minute incentive to subscribe, such as a discount or free shipping.

5. Engage with Existing Customers: Encourage repeat customers to join your email list by highlighting the benefits, such as exclusive offers and early access to new products. Include a subscription option during the checkout process or in order confirmation emails.

6. Partner with Influencers: Collaborate with influencers in your niche to promote your email list. Influencers can share your sign-up link with their followers, providing you with access to a broader audience.

Crafting Effective Email Campaigns

1. Understand Your Audience; Tailor your email content to the preferences and needs of your audience. Segment your email list based on demographics, purchase history, and engagement levels to send more personalised and relevant emails.

2. Create Compelling Subject Lines: The subject line is the first thing recipients see, so it needs to grab their attention. Use clear, concise, and intriguing subject lines that entice users to open the email. Personalization, such as including the recipient's name, can also increase open rates.

3. Provide Valuable Content: Focus on delivering value in every email. This could be in the form of product recommendations, educational content, exclusive offers, or industry insights. High-quality content keeps subscribers engaged and encourages them to look forward to your emails.

4. Use Engaging Visuals: Incorporate high-quality images, videos, and graphics to make your emails visually appealing. Visual content can break up text and make your emails more engaging. Ensure that your visuals are optimised for quick loading times.

5. Include Clear CTAs: Each email should have a clear and compelling call-to-action (CTA). Whether you want recipients to shop a sale, read a blog post, or follow you on social media, make sure the CTA stands out and is easy to follow.

6. Mobile Optimization: Ensure your emails are mobile-friendly, as a significant portion of users will open them on their smartphones. Use responsive design, readable fonts, and appropriately sized buttons to enhance the mobile experience.

7. Best and Optimize; Conduct A/B testing to determine which elements of your emails perform best. Test different subject lines, content formats, visuals, and CTAs. Use the insights gained to continuously improve your email campaigns.

Automation and Segmentation

1. Welcome Series: Set up an automated welcome email series to greet new subscribers. This series can introduce your brand, highlight popular products, and offer a special discount as a thank you for subscribing. A warm welcome can set the tone for a positive relationship with your brand.

2. Abandoned Cart Emails: Automate emails to remind customers of items left in their shopping carts. These emails can include product images, descriptions, and a link to complete the purchase. Adding a limited-time discount can incentivize customers to finalise their purchase.

3. Post-Purchase Follow-Up: After a customer makes a purchase, send a series of follow-up emails. These can include order confirmations, shipping notifications, and requests for reviews. You can also suggest related products to encourage repeat purchases.

4. Re-Engagement Campaigns: Identify inactive subscribers and create re-engagement campaigns to win them back. Offer special deals, highlight new products, or ask for feedback. If they remain unresponsive, consider removing them from your list to maintain a healthy engagement rate.

5. Birthday and Anniversary Emails: Celebrate customers' birthdays and anniversaries with special offers or discounts. Personalised emails that acknowledge important dates can strengthen customer loyalty and encourage purchases.

6. Segmentation for Personalization: Segment your email list to deliver more targeted and relevant content. Common segmentation criteria include:
- **Demographics:** Age, gender, location, etc.
- **Purchase History:** Frequency, value, and type of purchases.
- **Engagement Level:** Opens, clicks, and website behaviour.
- Preferences: Stated interests or product categories.

By tailoring your emails to specific segments, you can increase relevance and improve engagement rates.

7. Behavioural Triggers: Use automation to send emails based on customer behaviour. For example, send a follow-up email if a customer views a product multiple times but doesn't purchase it. Behavioural triggers can help you reach customers at the right moment with the right message.

Leveraging email marketing involves building a robust email list, crafting compelling email campaigns, and utilising automation and segmentation to deliver personalised content. Offering valuable incentives and using strategic opt-in forms can help grow your email list. Crafting effective email campaigns with engaging content, clear CTAs, and mobile optimization can drive higher open and click-through rates. Automation and segmentation enable you to nurture leads, recover abandoned carts, and engage customers with personalised messages at every stage of their journey. By implementing these strategies, you can maximise the effectiveness of your email marketing efforts and drive more sales for your e-commerce business.UTILISING

CONTENT MARKETING

Blogging for E-Commerce

Blogging is a powerful tool for e-commerce businesses to attract and engage customers. By providing valuable content, you can drive traffic to your store, build trust with your audience, and improve your search engine rankings. Here's how to effectively use blogging for e-commerce:

1. Identify Your Audience: Understanding your target audience is crucial for creating relevant and engaging blog content. Conduct market research to identify their interests, pain points, and preferences. Create buyer personas to guide your content creation process.

2. Keyword Research: Use keyword research tools like Google Keyword Planner, Ahrefs, or SEMrush to find relevant keywords and topics that your audience is searching for. Focus on long-tail keywords that are specific to your niche, as they often have less competition and higher conversion rates.

3. Create High-Quality Content: Produce well-researched, informative, and engaging blog posts that provide value to your readers. Address common questions and problems your audience faces, and offer practical solutions. Use a mix of content types, such as how-to guides, product reviews, case studies, and industry news.

4. Optimise for SEO: Implement on-page SEO best practices to improve your blog's visibility in search engine results. Include your target keywords in the title, headers, meta descriptions, and throughout the content. Use internal and external links to enhance the user experience and boost your site's authority.

5. Consistency: Maintain a consistent posting schedule to keep your audience engaged and returning for more content. Whether you post weekly or bi-weekly, consistency helps build trust and establishes your blog as a reliable source of information.

6. Promote Your Blog: Share your blog posts on social media, in email newsletters, and through other marketing channels to increase their reach. Engage with your audience by responding to comments and encouraging discussions. Collaborate with other bloggers or influencers in your niche to expand your audience.

7. Measure Performance: Use analytics tools like Google Analytics to track the performance of your blog. Monitor metrics such as page views, time on page, bounce rate, and conversion rates. Use this data to identify what works and what doesn't, and adjust your content strategy accordingly.

Creating Video Content

Video content is an engaging and versatile way to showcase your products, share valuable information, and connect with your audience. Here's how to leverage video content for your e-commerce business:

1. Types of Video Content: Create a variety of video content to cater to different audience needs and preferences. This can include:
- **Product Demos:** Show how your products work and highlight their features and benefits.
- **Tutorials and How To Guides:** Provide step-by-step instructions on how to use your products or solve common problems.
- **Customer Testimonials:** Share authentic reviews and experiences from satisfied customers.
- **Behind-the-Scenes:** Give a glimpse into your company's culture, processes, and team members.
- **Live Streams:** Host live Q&A sessions, product launches, or events to engage with your audience in real-time.

2. Quality Matters: Invest in good equipment and editing software to produce high-quality videos. Clear visuals and sound, good lighting, and professional editing can significantly impact viewer engagement and perception of your brand.

3. SEO for Videos: Optimise your video content for search engines by using relevant keywords in the title, description, and tags. Include a transcript or subtitles to improve accessibility and searchability. Host your videos on platforms like YouTube and Vimeo, and embed them on your website and blog.

4. Promote Your Videos: Share your videos on social media, in email campaigns, and on your website to reach a wider audience. Use engaging thumbnails and compelling descriptions to attract viewers. Encourage your audience to like, share, and comment on your videos to boost engagement and visibility.

5. Engage with Your Audience: Respond to comments and questions on your videos to build a community and foster relationships with your audience. Encourage viewers to subscribe to your channel and turn on notifications to stay updated with your latest content.

6. Measure Success: Track the performance of your videos using analytics tools provided by platforms like YouTube and Google Analytics. Monitor metrics such as views, watch time, engagement rate, and conversion rate. Use this data to refine your video content strategy and improve future videos.

Leveraging Influencer Partnerships

Influencer partnerships can help you reach a larger audience, build trust, and drive sales. Here's how to effectively leverage influencer partnerships for your e-commerce business:

1. Identify Relevant Influencers: Look for influencers who align with your brand values, have an engaged following, and cater to your target audience. Use tools like BuzzSumo, Influence.co, or social media platforms to find potential influencers in your niche.

2. **Build Relationships:** Start by engaging with influencers on social media by liking, commenting, and sharing their content. Establish a genuine connection before reaching out with a collaboration proposal. Personalise your outreach and explain how the partnership can benefit both parties.

3. **Set Clear Goals:** Define your objectives for the influencer partnership, whether it's increasing brand awareness, driving traffic, or boosting sales. Communicate these goals clearly to the influencer and ensure they align with their content style and audience.

4. **Create Authentic Content:** Allow influencers creative freedom to produce content that resonates with their

audience. Authenticity is key to successful influencer marketing. Provide them with the necessary information about your products and brand, but avoid overly scripted or promotional content.

5. Track Performance: Use unique tracking links, discount codes, or UTM parameters to measure the success of your influencer campaigns. Monitor metrics such as engagement, traffic, conversions, and ROI. Analyse the data to determine which influencers and content types are most effective.

6. **Long-Term Partnerships:** Consider building long-term relationships with influencers rather than one-off collaborations. Long-term partnerships can create more consistent and impactful results. Influencers can become brand ambassadors, regularly promoting your products and fostering trust with their audience.

7. **Compliance and Disclosure:** Ensure that influencers comply with advertising regulations and disclose their partnerships with your brand. Transparency builds trust with the audience and maintains the credibility of both the influencer and your brand.

Utilising content marketing through blogging, video content, and influencer partnerships can significantly enhance your e-commerce business. Blogging helps attract and engage your audience with valuable information, while video content provides a dynamic and visual way to showcase your products and connect with viewers. Leveraging influencer partnerships allows you to reach a wider audience and build trust through authentic and engaging content. By implementing these strategies, you can drive traffic, increase conversions, and grow your e-commerce business.

MANAGING CUSTOMER RELATIONSHIPS

Providing Excellent Customer Service

Excellent customer service is the foundation of any successful e-commerce business. It fosters trust, encourages repeat business, and can set you apart from your competitors. Here are key strategies for providing top-notch customer service:

1. Respond Promptly: Customers appreciate quick responses to their inquiries. Aim to respond to emails and social media messages within 24 hours. Live chat support can be especially effective for providing immediate assistance.

2. Train Your Team: Ensure your customer service team is well-trained and knowledgeable about your products and policies. They should be equipped to handle a variety of questions and issues efficiently and professionally.

3. Personalise Interactions: Personalization goes a long way in making customers feel valued. Address customers by their names, reference their previous purchases or interactions, and tailor your responses to their specific needs.

4. Be Proactive: Anticipate potential issues and address them before they become problems. For example, if there's a delay in shipping, inform your customers as soon as possible and provide updates until the issue is resolved.

5. Use Positive Language: The way you communicate with customers can greatly impact their experience. Use positive language, stay polite, and focus on solutions rather than problems. For instance, instead of saying, "We can't do that," say, "Here's what we can do."

6. Collect Feedback: Regularly solicit feedback from your customers to understand their needs and improve your services. Use surveys, follow-up emails, and direct conversations to gather insights and act on them.

7. Resolve Issues Efficiently: When problems arise, handle them quickly and effectively. Apologise for any inconvenience, offer a solution, and follow up to ensure the issue has been resolved to the customer's satisfaction.

Handling Returns and Refunds

Returns and refunds are an inevitable part of e-commerce, but how you handle them can significantly affect customer satisfaction and loyalty. Here's how to manage returns and refunds effectively:

1. Clear Return Policy: Develop a clear, straightforward return policy and make it easily accessible on your website. Include details about the return window, acceptable conditions for returns, and any associated costs.

2. Simplify the Process: Make the return process as easy as possible for your customers. Provide pre-paid return labels, clear instructions, and an online return portal if possible. The simpler the process, the more likely customers are to shop with you again.

3. Communicate Clearly: Keep customers informed throughout the return process. Send notifications when their return has been received, processed, and when the refund has been issued. Clear communication can reduce anxiety and improve the overall experience.

4. Be Generous: Where possible, offer generous return policies. For example, provide free returns, extend the return window during holiday seasons, or offer store credit for returns outside the regular window. Generosity in returns can build customer trust and loyalty.

5. Analyze Return Data: Use data from returns to identify common issues with products or descriptions. This information can help you improve product quality, refine descriptions, and reduce the return rate over time.

6. Train Your Team: Ensure your customer service team is well-trained to handle returns and refunds. They should know the return policy inside and out and be empowered to resolve issues quickly and fairly.

7. Turn Returns into Opportunities: Use returns as an opportunity to engage with customers and show them you value their business. Offer personalised recommendations for alternative products or provide discounts for future purchases.

Building Customer Loyalty

Building customer loyalty is crucial for long-term success in e-commerce. Loyal customers are more likely to make repeat purchases, refer others, and become advocates for your brand. Here's how to cultivate loyalty:

1. Loyalty Programs: Implement a loyalty program that rewards customers for their repeat business. Offer points for purchases, referrals, and social media engagement that can be redeemed for discounts, free products, or exclusive offers.

2. Exclusive Offers: Provide exclusive discounts and early access to sales for loyal customers. Making them feel special and appreciated can strengthen their attachment to your brand.

3. Personalised Marketing: Use data to personalise your marketing efforts. Send tailored recommendations based on purchase history, personalised emails on special occasions like birthdays, and offers that align with their preferences.

4. Engage on Social Media: Build a community around your brand on social media. Engage with your followers by responding to comments, sharing user-generated content, and running interactive campaigns. Social media engagement can foster a sense of belonging and loyalty.

5. Exceptional Products and Service: Ultimately, the quality of your products and service plays a significant role in building loyalty. Ensure your products meet or exceed customer expectations and continually strive to improve your offerings and customer experience.

6. Customer Education: Educate your customers about your products and industry through blogs, videos, and newsletters. Providing valuable information helps establish your brand as a trusted authority and keeps customers engaged.

7. Solicit and Act on Feedback: Regularly seek feedback from your customers and show that you value their opinions by acting on their suggestions. Implementing changes based on customer feedback demonstrates that you care about their experience.

8. Consistent Branding: Maintain a consistent brand image and message across all touchpoints. Consistency helps build trust and recognition, making customers feel more connected to your brand.

Managing customer relationships effectively involves providing excellent customer service, handling returns and refunds smoothly, and building customer loyalty. By responding promptly, personalising interactions, and proactively addressing issues, you can offer outstanding customer service. Simplifying the return process and communicating clearly can turn potential negative experiences into positive ones. Implementing loyalty programs, providing exclusive offers, and engaging customers through personalized marketing and social media can foster long-term loyalty. By focusing on these strategies, you can enhance customer satisfaction, encourage repeat business, and build a loyal customer base for your e-commerce business.

ANALYSING AND OPTIMISING PERFORMANCE

Key Metrics to Track

Tracking key metrics is essential for understanding the performance of your e-commerce business and identifying areas for improvement. Here are some crucial metrics to monitor:

1. Sales Metrics:
- **Revenue:** Total income generated from sales. This is the most fundamental metric for assessing your business's financial health.
- **Average Order Value (AOV):** The average amount spent by customers per transaction. It's calculated by dividing total revenue by the number of orders.
- **Conversion Rate:** The percentage of visitors who complete a purchase. It's calculated by dividing the number of purchases by the number of visitors and multiplying by 100.

2. Customer Metrics:

- **Customer Acquisition Cost (CAC):** The cost of acquiring a new customer, including marketing and sales expenses. It's calculated by dividing total acquisition costs by the number of new customers.
- **Customer Lifetime Value (CLV):** The total revenue expected from a customer over their lifetime with your business. It's calculated by multiplying the average purchase value, purchase frequency, and average customer lifespan.
- **Churn Rate:** The percentage of customers who stop purchasing over a given period. It's calculated by dividing the number of lost customers by the total number of customers at the beginning of the period and multiplying by 100.

3. Website Metrics:

- **Traffic:** The number of visitors to your website. This includes total visits, unique visitors, and the sources of traffic (e.g., organic search, social media, paid ads).
- **Bounce Rate:** The percentage of visitors who leave your site after viewing only one page. A high bounce rate can indicate issues with site content or user experience.
- **Page Load Time:** The time it takes for your website pages to load. Faster load times improve user experience and can positively impact SEO and conversion rates.

4. Product Metrics:

- **Inventory Turnover:** The rate at which inventory is sold and replaced over a period. It's calculated by dividing the cost of goods sold by the average inventory value.

•**Return Rate:** The percentage of products returned by customers. It's calculated by dividing the number of returned items by the number of sold items and multiplying by 100.

Using Analytics Tools

Analytics tools provide valuable insights into your business performance, helping you make data-driven decisions. Here are some essential tools to consider:

Google Analytics: A comprehensive tool that tracks website traffic, user behaviour, conversion rates, and more. Key features include:

•**Audience Reports:** Provides insights into demographics, interests, and behaviours of your visitors.

•**Acquisition Reports:** Shows where your traffic is coming from (e.g., organic search, social media, paid ads).

•**Behaviour Reports:** Analyses how visitors interact with your site, including page views, bounce rate, and time on site.

•**Conversion Reports:** Tracks goal completions, e-commerce transactions, and revenue.

2. **Google Search Console:** A free tool that helps you monitor and maintain your site's presence in Google search results. Key features include:

- **Performance Report:** Shows search queries, impressions, clicks, and average position in search results.
- **Coverage Report:** Identifies indexing issues and errors on your site.
- **Enhancements:** Provides insights into mobile usability, site speed, and structured data.

3. **Hotjar:** A tool that provides heatmaps, session recordings, and surveys to understand user behaviour on your site. Key features include:
   - **Heatmaps:** Visual representations of where users click, scroll, and move on your site.
   - **Session Recordings:** Videos of individual user sessions to see how they navigate your site.
   - **Surveys:** On-site surveys to gather direct feedback from visitors.

4. **Klaviyo:** An email marketing and SMS platform with robust analytics capabilities. Key features include:
   - **Campaign Performance:** Tracks open rates, click-through rates, and revenue generated from email campaigns.
   - **Audience Segmentation:** Provides insights into customer behaviour and segmentation for targeted marketing.
   - **Lifecycle Analytics:** Analyses customer journeys and identifies opportunities for engagement.

Continuous Improvement Strategies

1. Regular Audits: Conduct regular audits of your website, marketing campaigns, and overall business performance. Identify areas that need improvement and develop action plans to address them. Audits help you stay proactive and ensure your strategies remain effective.

2. A/B Testing: Implement A/B testing to compare different versions of your website elements (example, headlines, images, CTAs) and determine which performs better. Use the results to optimise your site for higher conversions. A/B testing can also be applied to email campaigns, product pages, and ads.

3. Customer Feedback: Collect and analyse customer feedback through surveys, reviews, and direct interactions. Use this feedback to understand customer needs, preferences, and pain points. Implement changes based on the insights gained to improve customer satisfaction and loyalty.

4. Performance Benchmarks: Set performance benchmarks based on industry standards and past performance. Regularly compare your metrics against these benchmarks to gauge progress and identify areas for improvement. Adjust your strategies as needed to meet or exceed these benchmarks.

5. Competitor Analysis: Monitor your competitors' performance and strategies. Identify their strengths and weaknesses, and look for opportunities to differentiate your business. Use tools like SEMrush, Ahrefs, and SpyFu to track competitors' SEO, PPC, and content marketing efforts.

6. Training and Development: Invest in training and development for your team. Keep them updated with the latest industry trends, tools, and best practices. A knowledgeable and skilled team can drive better performance and innovation.

7. Scalability: As your business grows, ensure your systems and processes can scale effectively. Regularly review and optimise your operations to handle increased traffic, sales, and customer inquiries without compromising quality.

8. Data-Driven Decision Making: Base your decisions on data and analytics rather than intuition. Use the insights gained from your analytics tools to make informed decisions about marketing, product development, and customer service. Data-driven decision-making leads to more effective and efficient strategies.

Analysing and optimising performance involves tracking key metrics, using analytics tools, and implementing continuous improvement strategies. By monitoring sales, customer, website, and product metrics, you can gain valuable insights into your business performance. Tools like Google Analytics, Google Search Console,

Hotjar, and Klaviyo provide detailed data to guide your decisions. Regular audits, A/B testing, customer feedback, performance benchmarks, competitor analysis, team training, scalability, and data-driven decision-making are essential for continuous improvement. By focusing on these areas, you can optimise your e-commerce business for sustained growth and success.

SCALING YOUR BUSINESS

Scaling an e-commerce business involves strategic planning and execution to ensure sustainable growth. Key strategies include expanding your product line, entering new markets, and leveraging outsourcing and automation. Here's how to implement these strategies effectively.

Expanding Your Product Line

Expanding your product line can attract new customers and increase sales from existing ones. Here's how to do it:

1. Market Research: Conduct thorough market research to identify gaps in the market and understand customer needs. Use tools like Google Trends, social media insights, and competitor analysis to gather data on trending products and customer preferences.

2. Customer Feedback: Collect feedback from your existing customers to understand their needs and preferences. Use surveys, reviews, and direct interactions to gather insights. Consider offering new products that complement your current offerings.

3. Test New Products: Before fully committing to a new product line, test it on a smaller scale. Launch a limited edition or pre-sale to gauge interest and gather feedback. This approach minimises risk and allows you to refine your product based on customer responses.

4. Quality and Branding: Ensure new products align with your brand's quality standards and image. Consistency in quality and branding helps build trust and loyalty among your customers.

5. Supplier Relationships: Establish strong relationships with reliable suppliers to ensure the quality and timely delivery of new products. Negotiate favourable terms and maintain open communication to avoid supply chain disruptions.

6. Marketing Strategy: Develop a marketing strategy to promote your new product line. Use email marketing, social media, and paid ads to create buzz and drive traffic to your site. Highlight the benefits and unique features of the new products.

Entering New Markets

Entering new markets can significantly expand your customer base and revenue. Here's how to approach this:

1. Market Analysis: Conduct a thorough analysis of potential new markets. Consider factors such as market size, competition, cultural differences, and purchasing power. Use market research reports, industry publications, and local insights to gather data.

2. Localization: Adapt your products, marketing, and customer service to fit the local culture and preferences. This includes translating your website and marketing materials, offering local payment options, and considering local shipping and logistics.

3. Regulatory Compliance: Ensure you understand and comply with local laws and regulations. This includes product standards, import/export regulations, taxes, and data protection laws. Consulting with local legal experts can help navigate these complexities.

4. Partnerships: Establish partnerships with local businesses, influencers, or distributors. Local partners can provide valuable insights and help you navigate the market more effectively. They can also help with marketing, distribution, and customer service.

5. Pilot Launch: Start with a pilot launch to test the waters in the new market. This allows you to identify any challenges and refine your approach before a full-scale launch. Gather feedback from early customers and make necessary adjustments.

6. Scalable Infrastructure: Ensure your infrastructure can handle the increased demand from new markets. This includes your website, inventory management, and customer service capabilities. Invest in scalable solutions to support growth.

Outsourcing and Automation

Outsourcing and automation can help you manage growth efficiently and focus on core business activities. Here's how to leverage them:

1. Identify Tasks to Outsource: Determine which tasks can be outsourced to free up your time and resources. Common tasks to outsource include customer service, order fulfilment, accounting, and digital marketing. Focus on areas where external expertise can add value.

2. Choose the Right Partners: Select reliable outsourcing partners with a proven track record. Consider their experience, reputation, and ability to scale with your business. Establish clear communication channels and set expectations for quality and performance.

3. Automation Tools: Implement automation tools to streamline repetitive tasks. Use tools like Zapier, HubSpot, or Shopify apps to automate processes such as email marketing, social media posting, inventory management, and order processing.

4. Efficiency and Accuracy: Automation improves efficiency and accuracy by reducing human error and speeding up processes. This allows you to handle more orders and provide a better customer experience without increasing your workload.

5. Focus on Core Activities: Outsourcing and automation allow you to focus on core activities that drive growth, such as product development, strategic planning, and customer engagement. This strategic focus can lead to more innovative and effective business decisions.

6. Monitor and Adjust: Continuously monitor the performance of your outsourcing partners and automation tools. Gather feedback, track metrics, and make necessary adjustments to ensure they continue to meet your business needs. Regularly review contracts and performance to ensure you are getting the best value.

Scaling your e-commerce business requires strategic planning and execution. By expanding your product line, you can attract new customers and increase your sales from existing ones. Entering into new markets allows you to tap into new revenue streams and grow your customer base. Leveraging outsourcing and automation helps you to manage growth efficiently and focus on core business activities. Implement these strategies thoughtfully, and you'll be well on your way to sustainable growth and long-term success.

LEGAL AND FINANCIAL CONSIDERATIONS

Running an e-commerce business involves navigating a range of legal and financial considerations. Ensuring compliance with e-commerce laws, managing finances and taxes effectively, and protecting your business from legal risks are crucial steps for long-term success. Here's how to handle these aspects efficiently.

Understanding E-Commerce Law

E-commerce laws are designed to regulate online business activities, protect consumers, and ensure fair trading practices. Here are key legal areas you need to be aware of:

1. Business Structure and Registration: Choose a suitable business structure (sole proprietorship, partnership, LLC, corporation) based on your needs. Register your business with the appropriate government authorities and obtain necessary licences and permits.

2. Consumer Protection Laws: These laws ensure fair treatment of consumers and include regulations on advertising, product safety, and refunds. Familiarise yourself with laws like the Federal Trade Commission (FTC) Act in the US, which prohibits deceptive advertising practices.

3. Data Privacy and Security: Protecting customer data is paramount. Comply with data protection laws like the General Data Protection Regulation (GDPR) in the EU or the California Consumer Privacy Act (CCPA) in the US. Implement secure data handling practices, such as encryption and secure payment gateways, to protect sensitive information.

4. Intellectual Property (IP) Rights: Respect intellectual property rights to avoid legal disputes. Ensure you have the right to use all images, logos, and content on your website. Register your trademarks and copyrights to protect your brand and content from infringement.

5. Terms and Conditions: Draft clear and comprehensive terms and conditions for your website. This document should outline the rules and guidelines for using your site, return policies, and limitations of liability. Make sure customers agree to these terms before making a purchase.

6. International Trade Laws: If you sell internationally, be aware of trade laws and regulations in different countries. This includes customs regulations, import/export restrictions, and compliance with local consumer protection laws.

Managing Finances and Taxes

Efficient financial management and tax compliance are critical for the sustainability of your e-commerce business. Here's how to manage these aspects:

1. Accounting System: Set up a robust accounting system to track income, expenses, and profits. Use accounting software like QuickBooks, Xero, or FreshBooks to automate financial processes and maintain accurate records.

2. Budgeting and Forecasting: Create a budget to manage your business finances effectively. Regularly update your financial forecasts based on sales trends, market conditions, and business goals. This helps in making informed financial decisions and planning for growth.

3. Cash Flow Management: Maintain a healthy cash flow by monitoring your income and expenses closely. Ensure you have sufficient cash reserves to cover operating expenses, inventory purchases, and unexpected costs. Consider offering multiple payment options to facilitate faster payments from customers.

4. Tax Compliance: Understand your tax obligations and ensure timely filing of returns. This includes sales tax, income tax, and any other relevant taxes. Use tax software or consult with a tax professional to ensure compliance and take advantage of available deductions.

5. Financial Statements: Regularly prepare and review financial statements, including income statements, balance sheets, and cash flow statements. These documents provide insights into your business's financial health and help identify areas for improvement.

6. Funding Options: Explore funding options to support business growth. This can include loans, lines of credit, or equity investment. Evaluate the terms and conditions of each option and choose the one that aligns with your business needs.

Protecting Your Business

Protecting your e-commerce business from legal and financial risks is essential for long-term success. Here's how to safeguard your business:

1. Insurance: Obtain appropriate insurance coverage to protect against potential risks. Common types of insurance for e-commerce businesses include general liability insurance, product liability insurance, and cyber liability insurance. Consult with an insurance professional to determine the best coverage for your needs.

2. Legal Counsel: Establish a relationship with a legal advisor who can provide guidance on compliance, contracts, and dispute resolution. Having access to legal expertise can help prevent and address legal issues effectively.

3. Cybersecurity: Implement robust cybersecurity measures to protect your website and customer data from cyber threats. This includes using secure hosting, SSL certificates, regular security audits, and employee training on cybersecurity best practices.

4. Contract Management: Ensure all contracts with suppliers, partners, and service providers are clear and legally binding. Review contracts carefully and seek legal advice if needed to understand the terms and avoid unfavourable conditions.

5. Dispute Resolution: Develop a clear process for handling customer disputes and complaints. Aim to resolve issues amicably and fairly to maintain customer trust and avoid legal action. Consider using mediation or arbitration for resolving more complex disputes.

6. Compliance Audits: Conduct regular compliance audits to ensure adherence to legal and regulatory requirements. This helps identify potential issues early and implement corrective actions to avoid penalties and legal disputes.

Understanding e-commerce law, managing finances and taxes efficiently, and protecting your business from legal risks are essential for running a successful e-commerce business. Familiarise yourself with relevant laws, maintain accurate financial records, and implement robust security measures. By taking these steps, you can ensure compliance, financial stability, and long-term growth for your e-commerce venture.

CASE STUDIES AND SUCCESS STORIES

Real-Life Examples of E-Commerce Success

1. Amazon

Amazon started as an online bookstore in 1994 and has grown into the largest e-commerce platform in the world. Jeff Bezos, its founder, had a vision of creating a customer-centric company. Amazon's success can be attributed to its relentless focus on customer experience, a vast selection of products, competitive pricing, and fast delivery. The company introduced innovations such as one-click shopping, personalised recommendations, and Amazon Prime, which significantly enhanced customer loyalty and repeat purchases. Amazon's commitment to continuous improvement and expansion into various product categories and services (e.g., Amazon Web Services, Kindle) has solidified its position as a market leader.

2. Shopify

Shopify, founded in 2006 by Tobias Lütke, Daniel Weinand, and Scott Lake, is a leading e-commerce platform that allows businesses to create online stores.

The idea was born out of the founders' frustration with existing e-commerce solutions while trying to sell snowboarding equipment online. Shopify's success is driven by its user-friendly interface, extensive range of customizable themes, and powerful features that cater to both small businesses and large enterprises. By empowering entrepreneurs to set up and manage their online stores with ease, Shopify has grown rapidly and now powers over a million businesses worldwide.

3. Warby Parker

Warby Parker, founded in 2010 by Neil Blumenthal, Andrew Hunt, David Gilboa, and Jeffrey Raider, disrupted the eyewear industry with its direct-to-consumer model. By cutting out intermediaries and selling stylish prescription glasses online at affordable prices, Warby Parker was able to offer significant cost savings to customers. Their innovative Home Try-On program, which allows customers to try five frames at home for free before making a purchase, helped build trust and convenience. Warby Parker's commitment to social responsibility, including donating a pair of glasses for every pair sold, has also resonated with consumers, contributing to its success.

4. Glossier

Glossier, founded by Emily Weiss in 2014, is a beauty brand that grew out of a popular beauty blog, Into The Gloss. Weiss leveraged her blog's loyal following and insights into what consumers wanted to create a line of skincare and makeup products that prioritise simplicity and effectiveness. Glossier's success is largely attributed to its strong community engagement and direct feedback from customers, which informed product development and marketing strategies. The brand's minimalistic packaging, relatable marketing, and emphasis on customer experience have helped it build a devoted customer base and achieve rapid growth.

5. Dollar Shave Club

Dollar Shave Club, founded by Michael Dubin and Mark Levine in 2011, revolutionised the shaving industry with its subscription-based model. By offering high-quality razors and grooming products delivered directly to customers' doors at a fraction of the cost of traditional brands, Dollar Shave Club attracted a large customer base. The company's humorous and viral marketing campaigns, including the famous "Our Blades Are F***ing Great" video, helped it gain widespread recognition. In 2016, Dollar Shave Club was acquired by Unilever for $1 billion, showcasing the potential of innovative e-commerce models.

Lessons Learned from Top Entrepreneurs

1. Customer-Centric Approach: Successful e-commerce businesses prioritise customer satisfaction. Amazon's focus on customer experience, from fast delivery to personalised recommendations, has been a key factor in its growth. Entrepreneurs should listen to customer feedback, continuously improve their offerings, and ensure a seamless shopping experience.

2. Innovative Business Models: Disruptive business models can create significant opportunities. Warby Parker and Dollar Shave Club challenged traditional industries with direct-to-consumer and subscription models, offering better value and convenience to customers. Entrepreneurs should look for ways to innovate and differentiate their businesses from competitors.

3. Strong Brand Identity: Building a strong brand identity is crucial. Glossier and Warby Parker have succeeded by creating brands that resonate with their target audiences. Consistent branding, storytelling, and community engagement help build loyalty and trust. Entrepreneurs should focus on creating a compelling brand narrative and engaging with their customers authentically.

4. Leveraging Technology: Effective use of technology can drive growth. Shopify's success is largely due to its robust and user-friendly platform that empowers businesses to create and manage online stores. Entrepreneurs should invest in the right technology and tools to streamline operations, enhance the customer experience, and scale their businesses.

5. Agility and Adaptability: The ability to adapt to changing market conditions is vital. Successful entrepreneurs like Emily Weiss of Glossier have shown agility by pivoting and responding to consumer needs quickly. Staying informed about industry trends, being open to change, and iterating on products and strategies can help businesses stay competitive.

6. Community Engagement: Building a community around your brand can drive loyalty and advocacy. Glossier's direct engagement with its audience through social media and its blog has been a key driver of its success. Entrepreneurs should foster a sense of community, encourage user-generated content, and actively engage with their customers.

Case studies of successful e-commerce businesses like Amazon, Shopify, Warby Parker, Glossier, and Dollar Shave Club offer a valuable lessons for entrepreneurs. Focusing on customer satisfaction, innovating business models, building strong brands, leveraging technology, staying agile, and engaging with the community are key strategies for achieving e-commerce success. By learning from these examples, entrepreneurs can navigate the challenges of the e-commerce landscape and build thriving businesses.

CONCLUSION

Recap of Key Takeaways

Building and scaling a successful e-commerce business requires a strategic approach that encompasses various essential aspects. Here are the key takeaways from our exploration of e-commerce mastery:

1. Understanding the E-Commerce Landscape: The rapid growth of e-commerce presents significant opportunities, but also challenges that require a thorough understanding of market dynamics, customer preferences, and technological advancements.

2. Identifying a Profitable Niche: Conducting market research to identify underserved niches and crafting a unique value proposition can set your business apart from competitors and attract a loyal customer base.

3. Setting Up Your Online Store: Choosing the right e-commerce platform, designing an intuitive and attractive store, and using essential tools and plugins are foundational steps for creating a seamless shopping experience.

4. Product Sourcing and Inventory Management: Finding reliable suppliers, managing inventory efficiently, and choosing between dropshipping and holding inventory are critical decisions that impact your business's operations and profitability.

5. Creating Compelling Product Listings: Writing persuasive product descriptions, using high-quality product photography, and implementing effective pricing strategies can significantly enhance your product appeal and drive sales.

6. Building Your Brand: Developing a strong brand identity, creating a memorable logo and brand story, and maintaining consistent brand messaging are crucial for establishing trust and recognition among customers.

7. Driving Traffic to Your Store: Implementing search engine optimization (SEO), pay-per-click (PPC) advertising, and social media marketing can help attract and engage potential customers.

8. Maximising Conversions: Optimising the customer journey, using effective call-to-actions (CTAs), and conducting A/B testing are essential for converting visitors into paying customers.

9. Leveraging Email Marketing: Building an email list, crafting effective email campaigns, and using automation and segmentation can drive repeat purchases and foster customer loyalty.

10. Utilising Content Marketing: Creating valuable content through blogging, videos, and influencer partnerships can increase brand visibility, engage customers, and drive traffic to your store.

11. Managing Customer Relationships: Providing excellent customer service, handling returns and refunds efficiently, and building customer loyalty are vital for maintaining a positive reputation and encouraging repeat business.

12. Analysing and Optimising Performance: Tracking key metrics, using analytics tools, and continuously improving your strategies based on data insights are essential for sustainable growth.

13. Scaling Your Business: Expanding your product line, entering new markets, and leveraging outsourcing and automation can help manage growth and increase your business's reach and efficiency.

14. Legal and Financial Considerations: Understanding e-commerce law, managing finances and taxes effectively, and protecting your business from legal risks are fundamental for long-term success.

15. Case Studies and Success Stories: Learning from real-life examples and the experiences of top entrepreneurs provides valuable insights and inspiration for achieving e-commerce success.

Staying Ahead in the E-Commerce Game

The e-commerce landscape is constantly evolving, and staying ahead requires adaptability, innovation, and a customer-centric approach. Here are some strategies to keep your business competitive:

1. Embrace Technology: Stay updated with the latest technological advancements and integrate them into your business operations. This includes leveraging AI for personalised recommendations, using chatbots for customer service, and implementing advanced analytics for data-driven decision-making.

2. Focus on Customer Experience: Continuously improve the customer experience by offering fast shipping, easy returns, and excellent customer support. Personalise interactions and build strong relationships with your customers to foster loyalty and encourage repeat business.

3. Innovate Your Offerings: Regularly update and expand your product offerings to meet changing customer needs and preferences. Stay attuned to market trends and be willing to experiment with new products and services.

4. Optimise Marketing Strategies: Use a mix of marketing channels to reach a broader audience and engage with customers where they are most active. Regularly assess the effectiveness of your marketing campaigns and adjust your strategies based on performance data.

5. Invest in Employee Training: Equip your team with the skills and knowledge needed to excel in their roles. Regular training and professional development can improve productivity, foster innovation, and ensure that your business operates efficiently.

6. Monitor Competitors: Keep an eye on your competitors' strategies and performance. Understanding their strengths and weaknesses can help you identify opportunities and threats, allowing you to refine your approach and maintain a competitive edge.

Future Trends to Watch

The future of e-commerce promises exciting developments that can transform how businesses operate and interact with customers. Here are some trends to watch:

1. Mobile Commerce: With the increasing use of smartphones for shopping, optimising your online store for mobile devices is essential. Ensure a seamless and intuitive mobile shopping experience to capture the growing mobile commerce market.

2. Voice Commerce: The rise of voice-activated devices like smart speakers is changing how consumers shop online. Optimising your store for voice search and developing voice-enabled shopping experiences can give you an edge in this emerging trend.

3. Augmented Reality (AR): AR technology allows customers to visualise products in their environment before making a purchase. Implementing AR features can enhance the shopping experience, particularly for products like furniture, clothing, and accessories.

4. Sustainability: Consumers are increasingly concerned about environmental impact and prefer businesses that adopt sustainable practices. Emphasise eco-friendly products, reduce packaging waste, and communicate your commitment to sustainability to attract environmentally conscious customers.

5. Subscription Models: Subscription-based services are gaining popularity across various industries. Offering subscription options for your products can create a steady revenue stream and build long-term customer relationships.

6. Social Commerce: Social media platforms are becoming powerful e-commerce channels. Integrate social commerce features, such as shoppable posts and in-app purchases, to leverage the reach and engagement of social media.

7. Artificial Intelligence (AI): AI can enhance various aspects of e-commerce, from personalised recommendations and dynamic pricing to inventory management and customer service. Invest in AI technologies to improve efficiency and provide a superior shopping experience.

Navigating the dynamic world of e-commerce requires a strategic and adaptable approach. By understanding key elements of e-commerce, implementing effective strategies, and staying ahead of emerging trends, you can also build a successful and sustainable online business. Embrace technology, focus on customer experience, innovate your offerings, and keep an eye on the future to ensure your e-commerce venture thrives in an ever-evolving market.

Resources and Further Reading

To continue your journey in mastering e-commerce, it's essential to equip yourself with the right tools, expand your knowledge through additional reading, and take advantage of online courses and workshops. Here's a comprehensive guide to recommended resources that can help you enhance your e-commerce business.

Recommended Tools and Software

1. E-Commerce Platforms:

- **Shopify:** A popular and user-friendly platform for creating and managing your online store. It offers various themes, apps, and integrations to customise your store.
- **WooCommerce:** A WordPress plugin that transforms your website into a powerful e-commerce store. It's highly customizable and suitable for users already familiar with WordPress.
- **BigCommerce:** Known for its scalability, BigCommerce is ideal for growing businesses. It offers robust features and integrations for managing large inventories and high sales volumes.

2. Email Marketing Tools:

- **Mailchimp:** A versatile tool for creating, sending, and analysing email campaigns. It offers automation, segmentation, and A/B testing features.
- **Klaviyo:** Designed specifically for e-commerce, Klaviyo integrates with various platforms to provide personalised and automated email marketing solutions.

3. SEO and Analytics Tools:

- **Google Analytics:** Essential for tracking and analysing website traffic, user behaviour, and conversion rates.
- **SEMrush:** A comprehensive SEO tool that helps with keyword research, competitive analysis, and site audits.
- **Moz:** Another powerful SEO tool that offers keyword tracking, link building, and site analysis.

4. Payment Gateways:

- **PayPal:** Widely used and trusted, PayPal offers secure payment processing for online transactions.
- **Stripe:** Known for its developer-friendly API, Stripe supports various payment methods and currencies.

5. Customer Service Tools:

- **Zendesk:** Provides a comprehensive suite of customer service solutions, including ticketing, live chat, and knowledge base management.
- **LiveChat:** A real-time chat tool that allows you to assist customers instantly on your website.

6. Inventory Management Tools:

•**TradeGecko:** An inventory management software that helps you track stock levels, manage orders, and forecast demand.

•**Cin7:** Offers a range of features for inventory management, including automation, order tracking, and integrations with various e-commerce platforms.

Additional Books and Articles

1. Books:

•"**E-Commerce Evolved" by Tanner Larsson:** This book provides a comprehensive guide to building a successful e-commerce business, covering strategies for increasing traffic, conversions, and sales.

•"**The Lean Startup" by Eric Ries:** While not exclusively about e-commerce, this book offers valuable insights into creating and managing successful startups, emphasising the importance of innovation and adaptability.

•'**Building a StoryBrand" by Donald Miller:** This book helps you understand how to create a compelling brand story that resonates with customers and drives engagement.

2. Articles:

•"**The Ultimate Guide to E-Commerce" by Shopify:** A detailed guide covering everything from setting up your store to marketing and scaling your business.

•"**E-Commerce SEO: The Definitive Guide" by Backlinko:** An in-depth article on optimising your e-commerce site for search engines to drive organic traffic.

• "**The Complete Guide to Conversion Rate Optimization" by Neil Patel:** Offers practical tips and strategies for increasing the conversion rates of your e-commerce site.

Online Courses and Workshops

1. Coursera:

• "**Digital Marketing Specialization":** Offered by the University of Illinois, this series of courses covers digital marketing strategies, including e-commerce marketing, SEO, and social media marketing.

• "**E-Commerce Essential":** A course that covers the basics of setting up and running an ecommerce business, from product sourcing to marketing and analytics.

2. Udemy:

• "**Shopify Power: Building a Profitable E-Commerce Store":** A comprehensive course on setting up and optimising a Shopify store for maximum profitability.

• "**SEO for E-Commerce: The Complete Guide":** Focuses on strategies to improve the search engine ranking of your e-commerce site.

3. Skillshare:

• "**E-Commerce Essentials:** How to Start a Successful Online Business": This course provides step-by-step guidance on creating and growing an e-commerce business.

•**Email Marketing for E-Commerce":** Learn how to create effective email campaigns that drive sales and customer loyalty.

4. LinkedIn Learning:

•**E-Commerce Fundamentals":** Offers a solid foundation in e-commerce principles, covering topics like online business models, setting up a store, and marketing strategies.

•"Content Marketing for E-Commerce": Teaches how to create and leverage content to drive traffic and sales for your e-commerce business.

Investing in the right tools, continuously expanding your knowledge through books and articles, and leveraging online courses and workshops are essential steps for mastering e-commerce. By utilising these resources, you can stay ahead of industry trends, optimise your business operations, and achieve long-term success in the competitive e-commerce landscape.

Bonus:

As a special bonus for purchasing "E-Commerce Mastery," you'll receive free access to an exclusive E-Commerce Marketing Calendar Template. This detailed and customizable template is designed to help you plan, execute, and track your marketing activities throughout the year, ensuring you stay organised and on top of your promotional efforts.

Benefits of the E-Commerce Marketing Calendar Template:

1. Comprehensive Planning:
  -**Monthly and Weekly Views:** The template includes both monthly and weekly views, allowing you to plan your marketing activities in detail and see an overview of your entire strategy at a glance.
  -**Seasonal and Holiday Promotions:** It comes pre-filled with major holidays and e-commerce events, so you can easily plan special promotions and sales campaigns around key dates.

2. Task Management:
  -**Detailed Task Lists:** Each month and week section includes detailed task lists for all your marketing

activities, such as content creation, social media posts, email campaigns, and advertising efforts.

-**Priority Levels:** Assign priority levels to tasks to ensure that critical activities are completed on time.

3. Content Scheduling:

-**Content Calendar:** Schedule your blog posts, social media updates, email newsletters, and other content marketing activities with ease.

-**Content Ideas:** Space for brainstorming and jotting down content ideas to keep your marketing fresh and engaging.

4. Campaign Tracking:

-**Marketing Campaign Planner:** Plan and track the details of each marketing campaign, including goals, target audience, budget, and key performance indicators (KPIs).

-**Performance Review:** At the end of each month, review the performance of your campaigns and adjust your strategy based on what worked and what didn't for you.

5. Collaboration and Sharing:

-**Team Collaboration:** If you are working with a team, the template allows for easy collaboration. Assign tasks, set deadlines, and share updates with team members.

-**Cloud Access:** Save the template to the cloud for easy access from anywhere and on any device.

6. Customization:

- **Customizable Fields:** The template is fully customizable, allowing you to tailor it to your specific needs and preferences.
- **Branding:** Add your brand colours and logo to make the template truly yours.

How to Use the E-Commerce Marketing Calendar Template:

1. Download and Set Up:
Upon purchasing the book, you'll receive a link to download the template. Open it in your preferred spreadsheet software (such as Microsoft Excel or Google Sheets).

2. Fill in Key Dates:
Start by adding important dates for your business, including product launches, sales events, and other key milestones.

3. Plan Monthly and Weekly Activities:
Use the monthly view to outline your high-level marketing strategy. Break it down into specific tasks and deadlines in the weekly view.

4. Execute and Track:
Follow the plan, execute your marketing activities, and use the tracking features to monitor progress and performance.

5. Review and Adjust:

At the end of each month, review the results of your marketing efforts. Use this information to adjust your strategy for the following month.

This E-Commerce Marketing Calendar Template is a powerful tool that will help you stay organised, maximise your marketing efforts, and drive consistent growth for your online business. It is designed to complement the strategies and insights provided in **"E-Commerce Mastery,"** making it easier for you to put theory into practice and achieve success.

E-COMMERCE MARKETING CALENDA

MONTH :	YEAR :

CAMPAIGN NAME	OBJECTIVE	START DATE	END DATE	BUDGET	KPI'S

TO DO LIST

- [ ]
- [ ]
- [ ]
- [ ]

EXTRA NOTES

E-COMMERCE MARKETING CALENDA

MONTH :

YEAR :

DATE	CONTENT TYPE	TOPIC	CHANNEL	STATUS

TO DO LIST

- ☐ _____
- ☐ _____
- ☐ _____
- ☐ _____

EXTRA NOTES

E-COMMERCE MARKETING CALENDA

MONTH :	YEAR :

DAY	TASK	ASSIGNED TO	DEADLINE	STATUS

TO DO LIST

- [ ]
- [ ]
- [ ]
- [ ]

EXTRA NOTES

E-COMMERCE MARKETING CALENDA

MONTH :	YEAR :

DATE	EVENT	GOALS	NOTES

TO DO LIST

☐
☐
☐
☐

EXTRA NOTES

THANK YOU !

Dear Valued Reader,

I am deeply grateful for your decision to purchase "E-Commerce Mastery." Your support means the world to me, and I am thrilled to have you as part of our community of aspiring e-commerce entrepreneurs. This book is written with the hope of providing you with valuable insights, practical strategies, and the inspiration you need to succeed in the dynamic world of online business.

Your dedication to learning and improving your e-commerce skills is truly commendable. It's this kind of commitment that drives innovation and success, and I am honoured to be a part of your journey.

Thank you once again for your support and trust in "E-Commerce Mastery." I am excited to see what you will achieve and look forward to hearing about your successes. If you ever have any questions or need further assistance, please don't hesitate to reach out. Remember, your success is my success, and I am here to support you every step of the way.

Warmest regards,

Alex Jordan

www.ingramcontent.com/pod-product-compliance
Lightning Source LLC
Chambersburg PA
CBHW072051230526

45479CB00010B/676